NAVY
SEALS

LEE SLATER

Checkerboard Library

An Imprint of Abdo Publishing
abdopublishing.com

abdopublishing.com

Published by Abdo Publishing, a division of ABDO, PO Box 398166, Minneapolis, Minnesota 55439.
Copyright © 2016 by Abdo Consulting Group, Inc. International copyrights reserved in all countries.
No part of this book may be reproduced in any form without written permission from the publisher.
Checkerboard Library™ is a trademark and logo of Abdo Publishing.

Printed in the United States of America, North Mankato, Minnesota
102015
012016

 THIS BOOK CONTAINS
RECYCLED MATERIALS

Cover Photo: www.sealswcc.com
Interior Photos: Andrew McKaskle/US Navy, p. 23; AP Images, p. 5; Joshua J. Wahl/US Navy, p. 22;
Kyle D. Gahlau/US Navy, p. 16; Mandy Hunsucker/US Navy, pp. 14-15; Roger S. Duncan/US Navy, p.
18; S.A. Thornbloom/US Navy, p. 14; Sam Shore/US DoD, p. 23; Shauntae Hinkle-Lymas/US DoD, p. 17;
Shutterstock, pp. 4, 8, 24-25, 29; United States Marine Corps, p. 25; US Army, p. 25; US DoD, pp. 6,
29; US Navy, pp. 7, 9, 28; www.sealswcc.com, pp. 8, 10, 11, 12-13, 26-27

Content Developer: Nancy Tuminelly.
Design: Anders Hanson, Mighty Media, Inc.
Editor: Liz Salzmann

Library of Congress Cataloging-in-Publication Data
Slater, Lee, 1969-
  Navy SEALs / Lee Slater.
     pages cm
  Includes index.
  ISBN 978-1-62403-971-3
1. United States. Navy. SEALs--Juvenile literature. 2. United States. Navy--Commando troops--
Juvenile literature. I. Title.
  VG87.S58 2015
  359.9'84--dc23
                          2015026597

CONTENTS

THE MOST
FAMOUS
MISSION

On September 11, 2001, **terrorists** attacked the United States. The attacks occurred in New York City, Washington, DC, and Pennsylvania. They killed 2,997 people and shocked the entire world. The attacks that happened that day are known as 9/11.

A group called al-Qaeda claimed responsibility for the attacks. Its leader was Osama bin Laden. For almost ten years, the United States military and intelligence communities

The World Trade Center's South Tower *(left)* was attacked second, but collapsed first.

searched for Osama bin Laden. In the spring of 2011, their efforts finally paid off. It looked like Osama bin Laden's hiding place had been discovered! He was in Abbottabad, Pakistan.

Now it was time for Navy SEAL Team Six to spring into action. Their mission was to "capture or kill Osama bin Laden." On May 1, 2011, 23 SEALs flew in two **helicopters** to the suspected hiding place. They arrived during the night.

Osama bin Laden

They wore night-vision goggles so they could see.

The compound had several buildings. The SEALs used explosives to blast a hole in the wall of a guesthouse. They searched it and then moved on to the main building. They found Osama bin Laden on the third floor. The SEALs shot and killed him. The world's most famous and feared **terrorist** leader was no longer a threat.

THE HISTORY
OF NAVY SEALS

During **World War II**, small units from the army and navy received special training. These groups formed in 1942 and were called Scouts and Raiders. They operated mostly at night and often underwater. These units had several jobs. Their members looked for safe landing places on shorelines. They guided boats into good positions for attacking the enemy. And they removed obstacles in the water or on shore.

In 1943, two other types of units were created for underwater missions. They were the Naval Combat **Demolition** Units (NCDU) and Underwater Demolition Teams (UDTs). Underwater obstacles could sink a boat or prevent it from reaching shore. To decrease this risk, the NCDUs removed man-made obstacles. The UDTs removed coral reefs. These teams also made maps of beaches.

The **Korean War** started in 1950, and the UDTs got **involved** again. This time their work was not limited to the water. They performed **raids** on land, blew up bridges and tunnels, and interfered with enemy movement.

In 1958, Admiral Arleigh A. Burke proposed creating new navy units for secret operations. These units would focus on **unconventional warfare**. These types of units weren't needed until the **Vietnam War**. US Navy SEAL Teams One and Two were created in 1962. Their members came from the already established UTDs. And so the Navy SEALs was born.

Navy SEALs in Vietnam

WHAT DOES SEAL STAND FOR?

The name SEAL is an **acronym**. It stands for sea, air, and land. These are all **environments** where Navy SEALs perform their missions.

SEA AIR LAND

THE INSIGNIA

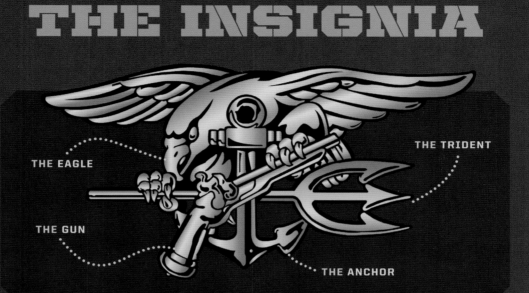

THE EAGLE

THE TRIDENT

THE GUN

THE ANCHOR

Each Navy SEAL receives a special badge. It is officially called the US Navy's Special Warfare **Insignia**. But most people call it "the SEAL trident" or just "the trident." The badge is gold metal and has four symbols on it.

- The anchor symbolizes the US Navy and the underwater units that came before the SEALs.

- The trident is a symbol of the ocean, where the SEALs began.

- The gun represents being ready to defend the United States.

- The eagle is the national symbol of the United States and represents freedom.

CHAPTER 3

ELITE
FIGHTERS

SEALs are an **elite** group. They are the toughest, smartest, most resourceful, and best-trained military men anywhere in the world.

SEALs perform a variety of difficult, dangerous, and secret missions. Surprise is one of their best weapons! SEALs can arrive from the water, air, or land. They fight the enemy using **raids**, **ambushes**, and assaults.

SEALs often work at night so they can sneak up on the enemy.

This SEAL's weapon is an M4 assault rifle.

SEALs are trained to collect information. They learn as much as they can about the enemy's activities. They also try to find out about enemy locations and the conditions on the ground. When it is time to strike, this information will help them succeed.

SEALs also train friendly foreign forces. They want to help make foreign soldiers better at responding to dangerous situations. Also, the foreign soldiers can help the SEALs collect valuable information.

Since 9/11, the SEALs have been **involved** in **counterterrorism**. They find and eliminate threats to the United States. If they learn that **terrorists** are planning an attack, they go after the group's leaders and members. The SEALs are also rescue experts. They rescue US soldiers and citizens captured by enemy forces.

ULTIMATE
TEAMWORK

Teamwork is the most important part of being a Navy SEAL. Every team member has a special job to do. A SEAL team has a strong bond. Its members have to completely trust and respect one another. A SEAL team will never leave a dead or wounded teammate behind.

A SEAL team is under the command of a navy commander. Each team includes ten 16-man **platoons** plus support

staff at headquarters. Each **platoon** has two officers and 14 **enlisted** men. A platoon can operate in groups of two, four, eight, or 16 men. The number depends on the mission.

In 2015, there were nine SEAL teams on active duty. There were also two Reserve Teams. The Reserve Teams are ready to help when they are needed.

The Navy SEAL Ethos expresses the beliefs that guide the SEALs. Part of it says, "My Nation expects me to be physically harder and mentally stronger than my enemies. If knocked down, I will get back up, every time. I will draw on every remaining ounce of strength to protect my teammates and to accomplish our mission."

SEALs doing immediate action drills as part of their training

EXTREME TRAINING

Navy SEAL training is very difficult. Only one out of five candidates who start it will finish. It takes extreme physical and mental toughness to become a SEAL.

Only men can apply to become Navy SEALs. A candidate must be between 17 and 28 years of age. He must be a US citizen and already

The Naval Special Warfare Preparatory School

enlisted in the US Navy. He undergoes special tests. The tests determine whether he has the mental and physical ability to become a SEAL.

Candidates who pass the tests go to the Naval Special Warfare Preparatory School in Great Lakes, Illinois. It is a two-month program. At the end, the candidates take a Physical Screening Test. The test is a 1000-yard (914.4 m) swim, 70 or more push-ups, 10 or more pull-ups, 60 or more sit-ups, and a four-mile (6.5 km) run.

Candidates have to complete the Physical Screening Test in less than an hour! Those who pass the test move on to BUD/S training. Candidates who fail the test can stay in the navy, but they cannot become Navy SEALs.

SEAL candidates swimming during the Physical Screening Test

BUD/S

BUD/S stands for Basic Underwater **Demolition**/SEAL. BUD/S training takes place in Coronado, California. BUD/S has three seven-week **phases**.

SEAL candidates training on the beach

The first **phase** is designed to make the SEAL candidates physically strong. Every day, they swim for hours and run for miles. They do hundreds of sit-ups and push-ups, and dozens of pull-ups.

SEAL candidates lift 600-pound (272 kg) logs.

The fourth week of training is called Hell Week. The goal is to push the candidates to their limits of physical and mental **endurance**. Over five and one-half days, the candidates sleep only about four hours! They run more than 200 miles. They do physical training for more than 20 hours a day. If a candidate wants to drop out, he can ring a bell at any time. During Hell Week, more than half the candidates drop out!

The second phase teaches combat diving and underwater skills. The third phase deals with land combat warfare training. This includes weapons, patrolling, and **marksmanship**. The men learn about **camouflage**, navigation, and how to move silently and without being seen.

Men who make it through BUD/S have shown amazing commitment, strength, and will. They still have a long way to go to become SEALs, but they are well on their way!

THE FINAL STAGES

After BUD/S, the next stage is SEAL Qualification Training (SQT). Candidates learn **demolitions**, medical skills, **parachuting**, and more. Before they can graduate, candidates go through Survival, **Evasion**, Resistance, and Escape (SERE) training. The navy wants SEALs to be well prepared if they are ever captured by the enemy.

During SERE training, a candidate is dropped off in the wilderness without food or water. He is then captured by instructors pretending to be the enemy. They treat the candidate like a prisoner. The candidate has three goals. He must not give up any information. He must escape if possible. And he must gather information about the enemy.

Finally, the candidate has earned the right to wear the SEAL trident. The pinning of the trident is a big moment in every SEALs life. Once the pin is on, watch out! It's a Navy SEAL tradition to throw the new SEAL into the ocean!

SERE training takes place in all climates.

TRAIN LIKE A SEAL

Before starting Navy SEAL training, a candidate has to pass a test of physical **endurance**. Some men train for up to a year to meet the **minimum** standards. It's not at all easy!

Navy SEAL Physical Screening Test (PST) Standards

PST EVENT	MINIMUM STANDARDS	OPTIMUM STANDARDS
500-yard swim	12 minutes and 30 seconds	9 minutes
push-ups	50	90
sit-ups	50	85
pull-ups	10	18
1.5-mile run	10 minutes and 30 seconds	9 minutes and 30 seconds

CHAPTER 8

A
DAY
IN THE LIFE

SEALs are always working to improve their skills and their physical strength and **endurance**. When the SEAL teams are not on a mission, a typical day might be like the schedule shown here.

If the SEALs are planning a mission, the day

MORNING

6 am	breakfast
7 to 9 am	**Team Physical Training (including swimming and running)**
9 to noon	**Team Skill Training (weapons, parachuting, diving)**

will be somewhat different. In addition to some physical and skills training, they focus on preparing for the mission. SEALs practice for their missions and test out different possibilities.

They consider a number of questions. How will we get there? How can we reach the target without being seen? What will we do when we get there? What if the **helicopter** crashes? What if someone gets captured? What if the **parachute** lands too far from the target? They talk as a team and plan for the best and the worst. Whatever happens, the Navy SEALs will be ready.

AFTERNOON

12 to 1 pm	lunch
1 to 5 pm	more Team Skill Training
5 to 6 pm	clean up
6 to 8 pm	discuss the day's work over dinner
after 8 pm	free time and then bedtime

AIR & SEA
VEHICLES

SEALs are most at home on and under the water. But they operate from the air and on land with expert skill too. For training and missions they use boats, submarines, **helicopters**, and airplanes. They also use other vehicles that have been specially designed for their needs.

Combat Rubber Raiding Craft (CRRC)

These rafts can be launched from large boats and submarines or dropped from helicopters. They can carry at least six men and are very fast and quiet.

SEAL Delivery Vehicle (SDV)

SDVs are launched from the backs of submarines. The SEALs get into them with all their SCUBA gear on. Then the SDV is flooded with water and shot out of the submarine.

Black Hawk Helicopter

These **helicopters** were designed especially for the US Army. They were first used in active service in 1978. Over the years, many changes have been made to improve the original Black Hawk. Today, Black Hawk helicopters have **silencers** so they can fly without making much noise. And some models have a special coating that makes them hard to detect on radar.

WEAPONS

A Navy SEAL is trained to use a variety of weapons. These include guns, knives, hand **grenades**, and their hands. Every SEAL is trained in **martial arts**. Their hands, feet, and bodies become deadly weapons!

submachine gun

anti-tank rocket launcher

handgun

assault rifle

SEALs never know what their next mission will require, so they have to be able to use many different weapons. One mission might **involve** shooting at targets in the distance. For this, a **sniper** rifle or rocket launcher could do the job. On a mission inside a house or compound, they might choose guns with short barrels. Hand **grenades** can be used to blast down gates and doors. When it comes to hand-to-hand combat, SEALs use knives or **martial arts**. A SEAL is trained to know what weapon to use in any situation.

combat shotgun

sniper rifle

THE FUTURE

OF THE SEALS

When the **terrorists** attacked on 9/11, it caught us by surprise. Today, Navy SEALs are working hard to stop terror attacks before they happen. Their missions are usually secret and always dangerous. Navy SEALs regularly risk their lives for their country. They help ensure that the United States is a safe place to live.

As new skills are needed in the future, some of the training will change. Ten years from now, SEALs might need skills that haven't even been imagined yet! Physical training will always be important.

Advances in **technology** will give the SEALs new tools and weapons. For example, a new Unmanned Underwater Vehicle (UUV) is like an underwater **drone**. It doesn't need a pilot

because it is operated by remote control. It moves and looks like a fish! Using the UUV on missions will cut down on the lives risked.

Navy SEALs are trained to be resourceful and adaptable. They have training, skills, physical and mental strength, faith in themselves, and their team. Whatever the future holds, the SEALs are prepared to take on any challenge. They're not quite superhuman, but almost! United States citizens, as well as people all over the world, are lucky to have them on our team!

SEALs wear white camouflage for missions on snowy mountains.

TIMELINE

1942

Navy and army soldiers are trained as Scouts and Rangers.

1958

Admiral Arleigh A. Burke recommends new navy units for unconventional warfare.

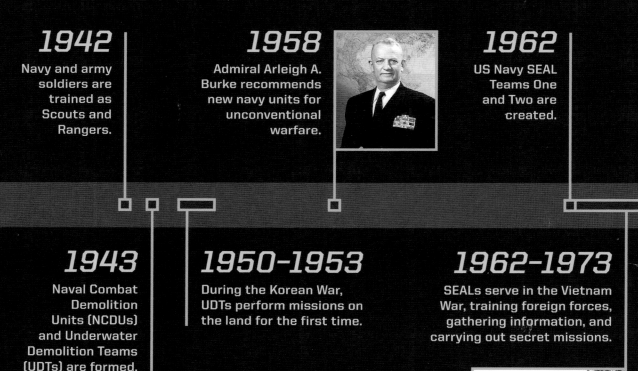

1962

US Navy SEAL Teams One and Two are created.

1943

Naval Combat Demolition Units (NCDUs) and Underwater Demolition Teams (UDTs) are formed.

1950-1953

During the Korean War, UDTs perform missions on the land for the first time.

1962-1973

SEALs serve in the Vietnam War, training foreign forces, gathering information, and carrying out secret missions.

2001

Terrorists attack the United States on September 11.

2011

Navy SEAL Team Six finds and kills Osama bin Laden.

EXTREME FACTS

- There are about 2,500 Navy SEALs on active duty in more than 30 countries.

- Someone who is **color-blind** cannot become a SEAL.

- A SEAL has to be able to hold his breath underwater for at least one minute.

- Navy SEALs make up less than 1 percent of the US Navy.

- The last line of the SEAL Ethos is "I will not fail."

GLOSSARY

acronym – a word made from the beginning letters of words in a phrase.

ambush – a surprise attack from a hidden position.

camouflage – relating to hiding or disguising something by covering it up or changing its appearance.

color-blind – partially or totally unable to tell one color from another.

counterterrorism – efforts and strategies to fight or prevent terrorism.

demolition – the act of destroying something, especially by using explosives.

drone – an aircraft or ship that is controlled by radio signals.

elite – of or relating to the best of a class.

endurance – the ability to sustain a long, stressful effort or activity.

enlist – to join the armed forces voluntarily. An enlisted man is a person who enlists for military service.

environment – surroundings.

evasion – the act of escaping or avoiding something.

grenade – a small bomb that is thrown by hand or shot from a gun.

helicopter – an aircraft without wings. Instead, it has blades that rotate parallel to the ground.

insignia – a symbol or design that indicates a special authority, office, or honor.

involve – 1. to take part in something. 2. to require certain parts or actions.

Korean War – a war fought in North and South Korea from 1950 to 1953. The US government sent troops to help South Korea.

WEBSITES

To learn more about Special Ops, visit **booklinks.abdopublishing.com**. These links are routinely monitored and updated to provide the most current information available.

marksmanship – the skill of shooting a target.

martial arts – an art of combat or self-defense practiced as a sport.

minimum – the least amount possible or allowed.

parachute – to jump out of an aircraft and use a parachute to fall slowly to the ground. A parachute is an umbrella-like device consisting of fabric from which a person or object is suspended.

phase – a step or stage of a process.

platoon – a type of military group.

raid – a surprise attack.

silencer – a device that quiets the sound of a firearm or aircraft.

sniper – someone who shoots at an enemy from a hidden place far away.

technology – scientific tools or methods for doing tasks or solving problems.

terrorism – the use of violence to threaten people or governments. A person who does this is a terrorist.

unconventional warfare – an attempt to achieve military victory through agreement, surrender, or spying.

Vietnam War – from 1957 to 1975. A long, failed attempt by the United States to stop North Vietnam from taking over South Vietnam.

World War II – from 1939 to 1945, fought in Europe, Asia, and Africa. Great Britain, France, the United States, the Soviet Union, and their allies were on one side. Germany, Italy, Japan, and their allies were on the other side.

INDEX

DATE DUE

3/15/17			
3-25-17			
			PRINTED IN U.S.A.